MORE
KENNEDY
WIT

MORE
KENNEDY
WIT

Edited by BILL ADLER

The Citadel Press   New York

Contents

The 1960 Campaign   13

The Presidency   51

The Family   79

The Press Conferences   91

MORE
KENNEDY
WIT

Books by BILL ADLER

THE KENNEDY WIT
THE CHURCHILL WIT
DEAR PRESIDENT JOHNSON
KIDS' LETTERS TO PRESIDENT KENNEDY

This is more of the Kennedy wit—that delightful humor and brilliant wit that all of us have come to associate with John F. Kennedy.

From his very first days in public office, as a young Congressman from Boston, John F. Kennedy showed that he had the rare gift of bringing laughter to others.

As his career developed and flourished from United States Senator to thirty-fifth President of the United States, his wit became a Kennedy trademark.

The material in this book has been selected from President Kennedy's speeches, press conferences, letters, conversations with family and friends, and remarks he made everywhere, from Massachusetts to Ireland.

Here is John F. Kennedy in his own words, as family man, Senator and President. Here is John F. Kennedy with that famous warm smile and unforgettable wit that were an integral part of this great American.

BILL ADLER

New York City
February 1965

THE
1960
CAMPAIGN

The
1960
Campaign

In 1958, there were many Democratic aspirants for the 1960 Presidential nomination. Among them were John F. Kennedy, Lyndon Johnson, and Stuart Symington.

Mr. Kennedy liked to tell this story about the scramble for the Democratic nomination:

Several nights ago, I dreamed that the good Lord touched me on the shoulder and said, "Don't worry, you'll be the Democratic Presidential nominee in 1960. What's more, you'll be elected." I told Stu Symington about my dream. "Funny thing," said Stu, "I had exactly the same dream about myself."

We both told our dreams to Lyndon Johnson, and Johnson said, "That's funny. For the life of me, I can't remember tapping either of you two boys for the job."

Mr. Nixon in the last seven days has called me an economic ignoramus, a Pied Piper, and all the rest. I've just confined myself to calling him a Republican, but he says that is getting low.

> *New York City*
> *November 5, 1960*

In Los Angeles during the 1960 campaign, Mr. Kennedy was facetiously asked, "Do you think a Protestant can be elected President in 1960?"
This was his reply:

If he's prepared to answer how he stands on the issue of the separation of church and state, I see no reason why we should discriminate against him.

In a speech before the Women's National Press Club, Arthur Larson, former Director of the United States Information Agency under President Eisenhower, suggested that Senator Kennedy switch his party allegiance and become a "new" Republican. This was Mr. Kennedy's reply:

One temptation to accept Mr. Larson's invitation to become a "new" Republican is the fact that I would be the first Senator in either party to do so.

Question: President Eisenhower has been a pretty popular President. How much of a factor do you expect him to be in this campaign?

Mr. Kennedy: Well, none of us are able to elect other people, unfortunately, in this country. But I do think he is a help to Mr. Nixon. I would be glad to have his cooperation, but I think he is already committed.

Hyannisport, Massachusetts
July 28, 1960

There is an old saying that a farmer votes Republican only if he can afford it. I don't think the farmer can afford to vote Republican in 1960. I think the farmer is in the position of the famous Mark Twain hero who rose rapidly from affluence to poverty.

Wichita, Kansas
October 22, 1960

I understand that Tom Dewey has just joined Dick Nixon out on the Coast, to give him some last-minute strategy on how to win an election.

New York City
November 5, 1960

Addressing a luncheon of Democratic women, candidate Kennedy joked:

I believe the Democratic Party can do the job best, and I come and ask your help in doing it. There's an old saying, "Never send a boy to do a man's job, send a lady."

Queens, New York
November 5, 1960

Last night we had a parade in Chicago for one million people. I said to Mayor Daley, "They are all going to be so tired from being in the parade that they won't be able to get up on Tuesday [Election Day]."

New York City
November 5, 1960

The 1960 Presidential primaries were very hectic and candidate Kennedy was always on the go, so much so that he used to tell his friends:

Caroline's first words were plane, goodbye, and New Hampshire, and she recently learned to say Wisconsin and West Virginia. Any day now she is expected to come out with Maryland and Oregon.

Ladies and gentlemen, this is the first time in fourteen years of politics that I have ever heard of a Democratic meeting and the Rotary Club joining together. I don't know whether it means the Democrats are broadminded or the Rotary Club is broadminded, but I am all for it.

Dayton, Ohio
October 17, 1960

Arriving in Wisconsin for his primary fight with Hubert Humphrey in 1960, Mr. Kennedy commented:

I am the first of an advancing army. By next spring the state will look like a college campus telephone booth.

I have been, in the last three days, in eight states, among them California, New Mexico, Arizona, Ohio, Illinois, Virginia, and the Bronx, the ninth state.

Concourse Plaza Hotel
Bronx, New York
November 5, 1960

Ladies and gentlemen: I said up the street that I am a former resident of the Bronx. Nobody believes that, but it is true. I went to school in the Bronx. Now, Riverdale is part of the Bronx, and I lived there for six years. No other candidate for the Presidency can make that statement.

Bronx, New York
November 5, 1960

I understand that Senator Goldwater sent a wire to Nelson Rockefeller a few days ago saying Arizona is in the bag. Well, it seems to me it is a mighty thin bag.

I was not aware that there had been an election here. Votes are not going to be counted until Tuesday, November 8th. Mr. Nixon has not got any votes yet, and neither do I. And I believe that if we keep working, we will just take Arizona right out of Barry Goldwater's bag.

In any case, we will make it easy for him to be a candidate in 1964. That is the least we can do for a favorite son.

Phoenix, Arizona
November 3, 1960

Dr. Topping, distinguished guests, ladies and gentlemen: I am delighted to be here again at this distinguished university. As a former student of political science at Southern California in the East, Harvard University, it is a pleasure to address this body.

University of Southern California
Los Angeles, California
November 1, 1960

I recognize that the struggle here is not easy. I know that Barry Goldwater sent a wire to Nelson Rockefeller saying that it was in the bag in Arizona. It is in the bag for Arizona like it was in the bag for the New York Yankees.

Phoenix, Arizona
November 3, 1960

Stars of the entertainment world applaud candidate Kennedy after a speech. Left to right, they are: Janet Leigh, Jo Stafford, Louis Prima, Milton Berle, and Stan Freberg.

Commenting on the fact that Harold Stassen had announced that he would seek the Governorship of Pennsylvania, Senator Kennedy remarked:

Mr. Stassen announces he will run for Governor of Pennsylvania. He has already been Governor of Minnesota. That leaves only forty-six states still in jeopardy.

While we meet tonight in the Golden Gate of California, the rescue squad has been completing its operation in the city of New York. Governor Rockefeller, Henry Cabot Lodge, Vice President Nixon, and President Eisenhower all rode up together. I thought it was very unfair not to have Barry Goldwater along.

We have all seen those circus elephants, complete with tusks, ivory in their head and thick skins, who move around the circus ring and grab the tail of the elephant ahead of them.

San Francisco, California
November 2, 1960

During most of the 1960 campaign, a Republican "truth squad" followed Mr. Kennedy around the country, making speeches in places where the Democratic candidate had spoken. Mr. Kennedy made reference to the "truth squad" when he quipped:

Now we have five days before this campaign is over. I cannot predict what is going to happen. The "truth squad" has been ditched. They told the truth once and they don't let them travel around anymore.

San Diego, California
November 2, 1960

During the 1960 campaign there was some criticism in Catholic quarters of Mr. Kennedy's efforts to show that he was not influenced by the Vatican. Commenting once to reporters about this situation, he joked:

Now I understand why Henry the Eighth set up his own church.

Mr. Nixon trots out the same old [farm] program. He has given it new names, Operation Consume and Operation Safeguard. But the words are the same, the melody is the same. Only the lighting and makeup are different.

La Crosse, Wisconsin
October 23, 1960

I shook hands coming over here tonight with some farmers—and how can you tell that they are farmers? It is because their hands are twice as big. I don't know what they do with them all day but they are twice as big because they work longer and harder than anybody, with the possible exception of candidates for the Presidency.

Grand View, Missouri
October 22, 1960

I want to pay tribute to what I hope will be the Congressman from this district, Congressman-to-be O'Rourke. He is a young man of courage, and even though this ticket may be overbalanced with Irish names —O'Rourke, Kennedy and McNamara—nevertheless, I hope you will support him.

Lansing, Michigan
October 14, 1960

Before the 1960 campaign, John F. Kennedy engaged Senator Hubert Humphrey in a very spirited campaign in the Wisconsin primary. Mr. Kennedy made reference to the primary when he returned to Wisconsin.

I can make one boast that no other Presidential candidate in history can make. I have spent more time in the Third District than any candidate for the Presidency since George Washington. I chased Hubert Humphrey all over this district and never caught him.

La Crosse, Wisconsin
October 23, 1960

I want to express my appreciation to you for your generous reception at four-thirty in the morning at the airport. Back east, the Democrats go to bed about nine o'clock regardless of what happens, so I was very impressed, and my appreciation goes to all.

Pocatello, Idaho
September 6, 1960

At a press conference during the campaign, Mr. Kennedy was asked his opinion of various labor unions. This was his reply:

I must say I hope I have normal courage as a politician and candidate for office, but I don't have quite enough courage to settle the dispute as to whether we should have craft unions or industrial unions. I will let you gentlemen settle that.

Portland, Oregon
September 7, 1960

I am the first candidate for the Presidency to actively campaign in the State of Alaska. There are three electoral votes in Alaska. I left Washington, D. C., this morning at eight o'clock. I have come, I figure, about three thousand miles per electoral vote. And if I travel eight hundred thousand miles in the next two months, we might win this election.

Palmer, Alaska
September 3, 1960

Governor Brown [of California] and I have been pushing a train all the way down from the Oregon border since yesterday morning and picking up olives, grapes, bananas, corn and one thing or another all the way down the rich state of California. I am reminded somewhat of an expedition which Thomas Jefferson and James Madison took in the 1790's, when they went on a botanical expedition up the Hudson River to find fish and flowers, and coming down the river they stopped in New York. They met Aaron Burr and the Knights of St. Tammany and they formed a link between the rural United States and the cities of the United States. They formed the Democratic Party.

Los Angeles, California
September 9, 1960

Ladies and gentlemen, I want to apologize for keeping you waiting. I was not playing golf. We were over in New Jersey, campaigning.

Wilmington, Delaware
October 16, 1960

I remember reading when I was in school that at a rally in Madison Square Garden when President Roosevelt was running for a second term they unfolded a great sign that said, "We love him for the enemies he has made." Well, I have been making some good enemies lately. I find it a rather agreeable experience.

New York City
September 14, 1960

On a number of occasions during the campaign Mr. Kennedy had trouble with public address systems. That is what happened in St. Paul, Minnesota, when he joked:

I understand that Daniel Webster used to address a hundred thousand people without any trouble at all, and without a mike, so it should be easy for us. However, we are a little softer than they used to be.

October 2, 1960

Speaking in the Bronx, New York, toward the end of the 1960 campaign, Mr. Kennedy remarked:

A reporter asked President Eisenhower about a month ago what suggestions and ideas Nixon has had, and the President said, Give me a week and I will let you know.

We have the good fortune to have a member of the crew who was on my torpedo boat in World War II, who lives in this area of East St. Louis.

I would like you to meet my friend Mauer. He was

on a merchant ship that got sunk in the Solomon Islands and then he had the bad fortune to then come on my boat, which also got sunk.

Belleville, Illinois
October 3, 1960

What are we going to do with the Republicans? They can point to Benjamin Harrison, who according to legend saw a man forced by the depression to eat grass on the White House lawn and had only one suggestion for him—that he go around to the back where the grass was longer.

Springfield, Illinois
October 3, 1960

There is a terrible rumor to the effect that this is a Republican community. I am sure it is not true. But it would be interesting to know how many Republicans we have here today. Will you hold up your hands? Let us see how many Republicans with an open mind we have got. Two. Well, there is some prospect.

London, Ohio
October 17, 1960

During the 1960 campaign, Mr. Kennedy received two gifts from loyal supporters in Pennsylvania. At the presentation ceremony, he quipped:

I want to thank you for the plates. We will try to find a suitable house for them. We are looking now. And the golf clubs—I will be all ready to be President!

New Castle, Pennsylvania
October 15, 1960

Senator Humphrey, Mrs. Roosevelt, Senator Lehman, Mayor Wagner, Governor Harriman, Senator Morse, Congressman Celler, Governor Williams, Senator Hart—whom have we omitted? So many chiefs are assembled with so few Indians, up here and in the audience.

You can tell who isn't running for office by that relaxed posture they assume up here. Hubert and I are the only ones on edge.

New York City
October 12, 1960

I am here to pay tribute to a great South Carolinian . . . the New York Yankees' Bobby Richardson. Apparently he is one Yankee who has your blessings, and I am here to gain them too.

Columbia, South Carolina
October 10, 1960

While on the campaign trail, Mr. Kennedy always attracted great numbers of very young people to hear his speeches. In Girard, Ohio, the audience was particularly young and he quipped:

If we can lower the voting age to nine, we are going to sweep the state.

October 9, 1960

Will Rogers once said it is not the original investment in a Congressman that counts; it is the upkeep.

Alton, Illinois
October 3, 1960

I want to give you the best two-horse parlay in the state of Kentucky today. That is Western Kentucky State College in the winter and the Democratic Party in November.

Bowling Green, Kentucky
October 8, 1960

During his political campaigns for the Senate in Massachusetts, Mr. Kennedy was fond of telling the story of the little old Irish lady whose husband passed away:

She came to the ward leader with the complaint that

the officials wouldn't accept the answer she gave to a question they asked her about her late husband, which was "What did he die of?" When the ward leader asked her what her answer was, the little old Irish lady answered, "Sure, and he died of a Tuesday. I remember it well."

Senator Humphrey, Governor Freeman, gentlemen: I want to express great appreciation to Hubert. As I told him this morning, having to run against him in a couple of states is like playing Ohio State and then having to play Harvard. It is much easier to play Harvard after you have played Ohio State.

St. Paul, Minnesota
October 2, 1960

In the U.S. Senate, we are given the responsibility of ratifying treaties and confirming Presidential appointments. The House of Representatives, however, is given far greater power. They are given the power to levy taxes and appropriate money.

So any time you don't like the way your money is being spent or what the taxes are, do not write to Senator Humphrey or me, but write to Congressman Karth.

St. Paul, Minnesota
October 2, 1960

At a political rally in Rochester, New York, the Democratic Party standard bearer quipped:

I am informed by someone with a long memory that

when another Presidential candidate, Mr. Thomas Dewey, came here in 1948, he said, "It is good to be ·back in Syracuse."

He didn't know where he was going or where he was —and I don't think the Republicans do today.

September 28, 1960

Speaking at a political rally in Lockport, New York, Mr. Kennedy was aware of the fact that the city's mayor was a staunch Republican. The mayor was in the audience when Mr. Kennedy made these remarks.

I understand, Mr. Mayor, that you are a member of another active party in the United States. I hope you won't feel I am abusing the hospitality of the city if I say a few good words on behalf of the Democratic Party.

September 28, 1960

At a political rally in Pennsylvania, Mr. Kennedy noticed that despite the fact that it was daytime, his audience was packed with young people.
As he began his speech, he remarked:

Governor Lawrence, ladies and gentlemen, does not anyone ever go to school in Erie?

Erie, Pennsylvania
September 28, 1960

Addressing a "Breakfast with Kennedy" rally, Mr. Kennedy remarked:

It always warms the hearts of the Democrats to see

contributors gathered in one room on an occasion such as this. I wish there were some other way to run a campaign, but this is what makes the mare go and this is what keeps us moving today from here to Buffalo and on through New York. You would not have wanted to have gotten a telegram from Albany saying we were stranded there.

Erie, Pennsylvania
September 28, 1960

Former President Harry S. Truman was not a staunch Kennedy supporter prior to the 1960 Democratic Convention. However, after Kennedy received the nomination, Mr. Truman threw his enthusiastic support behind the Senator from Massachusetts. During the campaign, Senator Kennedy visited Mr. Truman at his home in Independence, Missouri. He was asked at a press conference shortly after his visit, "How do the Kennedy-Truman ranks stand after your Missouri trip?"

Senator Kennedy: They are as one, I am glad to say. I hope that I can do as well as he did. He told me all about how he did it. I hope I will come out as well as he did.

Des Moines, Iowa
August 21, 1960

Every time I get to the middle of the day, I look down at the schedule and there's five minutes allotted for the candidate to eat and rest.

Commenting on his early days in the House of Representatives as a Congressman, Mr. Kennedy remarked:

We were just worms over in the House—nobody paid much attention to us nationally. And I had come back from the service, not as a Democratic wheelhorse who came up through the ranks. I came in sort of sideways.

During the 1960 campaign, candidate Kennedy always seemed to be hours behind schedule. He made reference to this in a Wyoming speech when he remarked:

I first of all want to express on behalf of my sister and myself our great gratitude to all of you for being kind enough to have this breakfast and make it almost lunch.

Cheyenne, Wyoming
September 23, 1960

I think the state of Iowa has an opportunity to continue the same kind of responsible government which Governor Loveless has given this state, when you elect Nick McManus the next Governor of the State of Iowa. I hope you will send a young man down there to represent this district. This ticket is well balanced—O'Brien, McManus and Kennedy.

I hope you elect Congressman O'Brien, and I don't hold his name against him.

Sioux City, Iowa
September 21, 1960

Ladies and gentlemen, this is the third year in a row that I have been honored by being invited to this steer roast, and I hope that it is going to be possible for me to come back next year in a somewhat different capacity.

Cleveland, Ohio
September 25, 1960

Question: Are you going to change West Virginia's diet from beans to strawberries?
Mr. Kennedy: I am told you raise the finest strawberries in the world, so I am for it. We will send a few cranberries down from Massachusetts.

Charleston, West Virginia
September 19, 1960

At a press conference in West Virginia, Mr. Kennedy was asked if he would speak slower, to which he replied:

You are talking to a Yankee now. I suppose that is what my accent sounds like down here.

Charleston, West Virginia
September 19, 1960

Question: I am for Mr. Kennedy. And may I visit you when you are the President of the United States in the White House? I have tried three times and cannot get in.
Mr. Kennedy: Let's meet outside and we will get it all set.

Charleston, West Virginia
September 19, 1960

Ten years ago, as a Congressman, I came to this city at one o'clock in the morning for a Democratic rally and you were all here then. I don't know whether you have left this hall in the last ten years, but only in this city could they get a turnout for a Democratic candidate at eight o'clock in the morning or at midnight. That is the kind of a Democratic city to have.

Jersey City, New Jersey
September 15, 1960

Speaking to the Protestant Ministerial Association of Greater Houston, candidate Kennedy remarked:

I want you to know that I am grateful to you for inviting me tonight. I am sure I have made no converts to my church.

Houston, Texas
September 12, 1960

This port, this city, has been a great launching site for ships, missiles, and planes, and you're about to launch me into orbit over Texas later this afternoon.

San Diego, California
September 11, 1960

Campaigning in sunny California on a rainy day, Mr. Kennedy quipped:

I want to express my appreciation to all of you for coming down in this valley sunshine and rain to say hello.

Merced, California
September 9, 1960

I am very grateful to be the guest of Eastern Carolina College. I understand that they have had a most rapid growth and now wish to play in the Southern Conference. I am scheduled to play in the Southern Conference, too, and find it somewhat difficult. I hope you have success and that I do well also.

Greenville, North Carolina
September 17, 1960

I want to express my appreciation to all of you for having come down to the station to meet us. Today we celebrate the one hundred and tenth anniversary of the admission of the State of California into the Union. It seems to me that the great story of California has come about because people were not satisfied with things as they were. They liked Massachusetts and they liked Ohio and they liked Oklahoma, but they thought they could do better when they came to California. I don't know why they felt that way about Massachusetts.

Modesto, California
September 9, 1960

I am confident that the people of this Congressional District will send back to the House of Representatives, with an overwhelming majority, Mrs. Green, whose perhaps least distinction has been that she has been the chairman of my campaign.

Portland, Oregon
September 7, 1960

Candidate Kennedy's wife was not able to accompany him on the campaign trail because she was expecting a child. Mr. Kennedy alluded to this fact when he said:

Ladies and gentlemen, first of all I would like to introduce my sister, who is representing my wife, who is otherwise committed.

Salem, Oregon
September 7, 1960

Mr. Kennedy was questioned during the 1960 campaign at a press conference in Seattle, Washington.

Question: Senator, do you feel that strong personalities, such as President Eisenhower and Governor Rockefeller, campaigning against you will be perhaps a severe handicap in your campaign?

Mr. Kennedy: No.

Question: Why?

Mr. Kennedy: I think that President Eisenhower is not running this year, and Governor Rockefeller was not nominated. I agree that President Eisenhower would be a strong candidate if he was running.

Question: Do you feel that some of this might rub off?
Mr. Kennedy: I don't know. We will know in November how much is rubbing off.

September 7, 1960

Ladies and gentlemen, I have been informed that the object in front of me is a model of a small potato grown in this county last year. I have been under the impression that it was a new Snark missile which was about to go in the State, but I am going to take everybody's word for it.

Presque Isle, Maine
September 2, 1960

Shortly after the start of the 1960 campaign, Vice President Nixon had to go to the hospital. Mr. Kennedy was asked about this situation at a press conference.

Question: Senator, did you say you were not going to discuss the Vice President until he is out of the hospital?
Mr. Kennedy: That is right.
Question: Does that mean no personal references in your speeches?
Mr. Kennedy: That is right.
Question: But will you resume?
Mr. Kennedy: Well, we will see what happens then. I may discuss some of the Republican shortcomings but not Mr. Nixon's.
Question: You are not going to mention his part in any of them?

The President accepts a portrait of Abraham Lincoln
from the National Association of Colored Women's
Clubs in 1962.

Mr. Kennedy: Unless I can praise him.
Question: Do you mean as long as he stays in the hos-
    pital he has sanctuary?
Mr. Kennedy: Yes, that is right. I may go there.

Washington, D.C.
September 1, 1960

Mr. Nixon may be very experienced in kitchen debates. So are a great many other married men I know.

Alexandria, Virginia
August 24, 1960

At a press conference during the 1960 campaign, Mr. Kennedy was asked: "What sort of qualifications would you look for in the man you would select for the next Secretary of Agriculture?" He answered:

First, I think he should have been at some part of his life a farmer. Secondly, I think he should live in the midwest United States. Thirdly, he should believe that his responsibility is to preserve the family farm and not liquidate it. Fourth, and finally, it would be helpful if he were a Democrat.

Des Moines, Iowa
August 21, 1960

At the 1960 Democratic Convention, both Senator Kennedy and Senator Johnson were active candidates for the Presidential nomination. Prior to the balloting, they both appeared before a joint meeting of the Texas and Massachusetts delegations.

I'm glad we're not going to put these speeches to a vote . . . after looking at the Massachusetts and Texas delegates today. Let me just say that I appreciate what Senator Johnson had to say. He made some general references to perhaps the shortcomings of other Presidential candidates, but as he was not specific, I assume he was talking about some of the other candidates and not about me. I have found it extremely beneficial serving in the Senate with Senator Johnson as leader. I think if I emerge successfully in this convention, it will be the result of watching Senator Johnson proceed around the Senate for the last eight years. I have learned the lesson well, Lyndon, and I hope it may benefit me in the next twenty-four hours. It is true that Senator Johnson made a wonderful record in answering those quorum calls, and I want to commend him for it. I was not present on all those occasions. No, and I was not majority leader. As Lyndon knows, I never criticized. In fact, on every occasion, I said that I thought Senator Johnson should not enter the primaries, that his proper responsibility was as majority leader, and that if he would let Hubert, Wayne, and me settle this matter, we could come to a clear-cut decision.

Prior to the 1960 Democratic Convention, former President Truman said at a press conference that Senator Kennedy was not his first choice for the Democratic Presidential nomination. Senator Kennedy was asked by the press to comment on Mr. Truman's remarks.

The last conversation to which he referred in Independence was less precise than that. He said we must all join together to secure the best man. I did not feel that on that occasion he was asking me to step aside.

In August, 1960, candidate Kennedy was invited to address an AMVET Convention in Miami Beach. However, his schedule did not permit him to appear in person, so he telephoned his address to the Convention.

I should inform you that we are running a small convention of the AMVETs in Detroit this morning, because sitting next to me is the Lieutenant Governor of Michigan, John Swainson, who is an AMVET. Sitting beside me is Pete Koubra who is former National Committeeman of the AMVETs from Michigan, and also Carol Kay, who is the President and Senior Vice Commander of the AMVETs. So we've got a convention going ourselves.

Mr. Chairman, ladies and gentlemen, it is nine in the morning and this will be a quiet, dignified speech.

Philadelphia, Pennsylvania
October 29, 1960

I would like to present to you my three sisters, who have been campaigning around the United States, and who came with us today for the end of the campaign—my sister Eunice Shriver, my sister Jean Smith and my sister Patricia Lawford . . . I think Mrs. Lawford got a better hand than the other sisters.

Hartford, Connecticut
November 7, 1960

THE
PRESIDENCY

The President coaxes a reluctant Lady Bird Johnson
to the microphone. The occasion is the return of
Vice-President Johnson to Washington after a trip to
Asia in 1961.

The
Presidency

Speaking to students at the University of North Carolina after he became President, Mr. Kennedy said that he did not propose to adopt "from the Belgian Constitution a provision giving three votes instead of one to college graduates—at least not until more Democrats go to college."

Dave Powers, one of President Kennedy's closest friends and aides, received a scroll from the President on his fiftieth birthday, which read:

"President's Special Award, Physical Fitness Program. Walking fifty miles per month from TV to refrigerator and back. Presented to Dave Powers on his fiftieth birthday. In recognition of your athletic ability in hiking to my ice box to drink my Heineken's."

President de Gaulle of France announced early in Mr. Kennedy's term in office that France had developed her

51

own nuclear force so that she could be independent of the United States. A short time after this announcement, the President accepted a loan of the "Mona Lisa" from the French Minister of Culture with these remarks:

Mr. Minister, we in the United States are grateful for this loan from the leading artistic power in the world, France. I must note further that this painting has been kept under careful French control.

And I want to make it clear that, grateful as we are for this painting, we will continue to press ahead with the effort to develop an independent artistic force and power of our own.

The New York Times, *a traditionally Republican newspaper, endorsed John F. Kennedy for the Presidency.*

After his election, the President was quoted as saying:

In part, at least, I am one person who can truthfully say, "I got my job through the *New York Times.*"

As President, John F. Kennedy opposed Federal aid to parochial schools. This stand caused much consternation in Catholic circles. Shortly after his education bill was proposed to the Congress, Mr. Kennedy quipped:

As all of you know, some circles invented the myth that after Al Smith's defeat in 1928, he sent a one-word telegram to the Pope: "Unpack."

After my press conference on the school bill, I received a one-word wire from the Pope: "Pack."

At a Gridiron Club Dinner in Washington a few years after he became President, Mr. Kennedy was in rare form. He used the occasion to comment humorously on the fact that Mr. Adzhubei, Premier Khrushchev's son-in-law, had made an unprecedented visit to Rome.

I have a very grave announcement. The Soviet Union has once again recklessly embarked upon a provocative and extraordinary change in the status quo in an area which they know full well I regard as having a special and historic relationship. I refer to the deliberate and sudden deployment of Mr. Adzhubei to the Vatican.

I am told that this plot was worked out by a group of Khrushchev's advisors who have all been excommunicated from the Church. It is known as Ex-Com.

Reliable refugee reports have also informed us that hundreds of Marxist bibles have been unloaded and are being hidden in caves throughout the Vatican. We will now pursue the contingency plan for protecting the Vatican City which was previously prepared by the National Security Council. The plan is known as Vat 69.

Speaking of the religious issue, I asked the Chief Justice tonight whether he thought our new education bill was constitutional and he said: "It's clearly constitutional—it hasn't got a prayer."

Gridiron Club
Washington, D.C.

Strolling through the White House grounds one day, the President looked admiringly at the revitalized White

*House gardens with their lovely petunias and ageratum
and commented:*

This may go down as the real achievement of this
administration.

*On his trip to Ireland, President Kennedy received hon-
orary degrees from the two leading Irish universities,
Trinity College and National University. Trinity is Eng-
lish and Protestant in tone and National University is
historically Catholic. After receiving his honorary degrees from the two universities, Mr. Kennedy quipped:*

I want to say how pleased I am to have this association with these two great universities. I now feel equally
part of both, and if they ever have a game of Gaelic
football or hurling, I shall cheer for Trinity and pray for
National.

June 28, 1963

I am deeply honored to be your guest in the free Parliament of a free Ireland. If this nation had achieved its present political and economic stature a century or so ago, my great grandfather might never have left New Ross and I might, if fortunate, be sitting down there with you. Of course, if your own President had never left Brooklyn, he might be standing up here instead of me. This elegant building, as you know, was once the property of the Fitzgerald family but I have not come here to claim it. Of all the new relations I have discovered on this trip, I regret to say that no one has yet found any link between me and a great Irish patriot, Lord Edward Fitzgerald. Lord Edward, however, did not like to stay here in his family home because, as he wrote his mother, "Leinster House does not inspire the brightest ideas." That was a long time ago, however.

It has also been said by some that a few of the features of this stately mansion served to inspire similar features in the White House in Washington. Whether this is true or not, I know that the White House was designed by Hobin, a noted Irish-American architect and I have no doubt that he believed by incorporating several features of the Dublin style he would make it more homelike for any President of Irish descent. It was a long wait, but I appreciate his efforts.

There's also an unconfirmed rumor that Hobin was never fully paid for his work on the White House. If this proves to be true, I will speak to our Secretary of the Treasury about it—although I hear this body is not particularly interested in the subject of revenues.

Irish Parliament
June 1963

President Kennedy greeted enthusiastic crowds in Galway, Ireland, with this quip:

How many of you have relatives in America whom you'd admit to? If you ever come to America, come to Washington and tell them, if they wonder who you are at the gate, that you come from Galway. The word will be out—it will be *Céad míle fáilte*, which means in Gaelic "a hundred thousand welcomes."

June 29, 1963

I can imagine nothing more pleasurable than continuing day after day to drive through the streets of Dublin and wave—and I may come back and do it.

Dublin, Ireland
June 29, 1963

The scene was Cork, Ireland and the visiting American President was in rare form:

I would like to introduce to you the pastor of the church which I go to, who comes from Cork, Monsignor O'Mahoney. He is the pastor of a poor, humble flock in Palm Beach, Florida.

June 29, 1963

At a gathering in Wexford, Ireland, Mr. Kennedy was presented with an engraved gold box. Expressing his gratitude, the President remarked:

I am proud to have connected, on that beautiful gold box, the coat of arms of Wexford, the coat of arms of the kingly and beautiful Kennedys and the coat of arms of the United States. That is a very good combination.

June 29, 1963

About fifty years ago, an Irishman from New Ross traveled down to Washington with his family, and in order to tell his neighbors how well he was doing, he had his picture taken in front of the White House and said, "This is our summer home. Come and see it."

New Ross, Ireland
June 28, 1963

On his trip to Ireland, President Kennedy visited a third cousin, Mary Ryan, who prepared an elaborate buffet in in his honor.

I want to thank all those who prepared this. It was a great effort on their part. We can promise we will come only once every ten years.

Duganstown, Ireland
June 28, 1963

I don't want to give the impression that every member of this Administration in Washington is Irish. It just seems that way.

City Hall
Cork, Ireland
June 28, 1963

Mr. Mayor, I would like to have you meet the head of the American Labor movement, whose mother and father were born in Ireland—George Meany, who is traveling with us.

And I would like to have you meet the only man with us who doesn't have a drop of Irish blood, but who is dying to: the head of protocol of the United States, Angier Biddle Duke.

Wexford, Ireland
June 28, 1963

When my great grandfather left here to become a cooper in East Boston, he carried nothing with him except two things, a strong religious faith and a strong desire for liberty. And I'm glad to say that all of his great grandchildren have valued that inheritance. If he hadn't left, I'd be working over at the Albatross Company.

Ireland
June 1963

A short time after the 1960 election, the President-elect met with one of his advisors, Stewart Udall, to discuss plans for the Inauguration. Mr. Udall suggested that Mr. Kennedy add a touch of culture to the ceremonies by inviting Robert Frost to speak. Said Mr. Kennedy:

Great idea. We'll do it. But with Frost's skill with words, people will remember his speech instead of mine. I think we'd better have him read a poem.

Hotel Carlyle
New York City
December 1960

At a dinner at the White House with friends, President
Kennedy jokingly said he doubted that Pope John was
all the press pictured him to be. He remarked:

You Protestants are always building him up.

My grandfather always used to claim that the Fitzgeralds were descended from the Geraldinis, who came from Venice. I have never had the courage to make that claim, but I will make it now, on Columbus Day in this state of New Jersey.

Newark, New Jersey
October 12, 1961

In a speech before 3,500 Democratic precinct workers in Chicago, the President remarked:

I just want to see who did it last November, 1960, and there they are. They said terrible things about you, but I never believed it. I hope you will do the same for Congressman Sid Yates. I understand that Mayor Daley plans to keep you locked up here until November 6th, then turn you loose.

October 1961

President Kennedy held a meeting in the White House for fifteen of the top Army Commanders from around the world who had returned to Washington for a Pentagon briefing. As the President gazed at the Army brass surrounding him, he joked:

I realize that it is entirely a coincidence that this meeting occurred at the time of the Army-Navy game.

November 1961

The President once took visiting Prime Minister Nehru

of India on a boat ride aboard the Honey Fitz *past the luxurious mansions of Newport, Rhode Island.*

As they passed the fashionable resort, the President turned to the Prime Minister and said:

I wanted you to see how the average American family lives.

Shortly after he became President, Mr. Kennedy asked Professor James Tobin of Yale University to come to Washington as a member of his Council of Economic Advisors.

"I'm just an Ivory Tower economist," Mr. Tobin told the President. Mr. Kennedy replied:

That's the best kind. As a matter of fact, I'm an Ivory Tower President.

Told by one of his aides that the millionth tourist during his term of office was about to go through the White House, Mr. Kennedy joked:

Will he be a Cuban or a freedom rider or a woman in shorts?

August 1961

Chairman Khrushchev has compared the United States to a worn-out runner living on its past performance and stated that the Soviet Union would out-produce the United States by 1970.

Without wishing to trade hyperbole with the Chairman, I do suggest that he reminds me of the tiger hunter who had picked a place on the wall to hang the tiger's skin long before he caught the tiger. This tiger has other ideas. We invite the USSR to engage in this competition which is peaceful and which could only result in a better living standard for both our people.

In short, the United States is not such an aged runner and, to paraphrase Mr. Coolidge, "We *do* choose to run."

Summer, 1961

June 3, 1961, marked the official meeting of the new American President and Premier Khrushchev in Vienna.

While discussing the ticklish question of a nuclear test ban, the President quoted an old Chinese proverb to Premier Khrushchev:

"The journey of a thousand miles begins with one step."

"You seem to know the Chinese very well," Premier Khrushchev commented.

"We may both get to know them better," answered Mr. Kennedy.

While on a state visit to Canada, the President met the wife of Canada's Defense Production Minister, Raymond O'Hurley, who told the President that all her relatives in Ohio and Connecticut had voted for him.

The President smiled and remarked:

Well, with a name like O'Hurley, they should.

June 1961

Despite the disaster of the Bay of Pigs invasion, a Gallup Poll taken shortly after revealed that the President's popularity was higher than ever and that he registered favorably with 83% of those interviewed.

Upon learning this news, Mr. Kennedy exclaimed:

My God, it's as bad as Eisenhower.

Washington, D. C.
April 1961

On his first trip to Paris in June, 1961, the President addressed the employees of the U.S. Embassy and remarked:

I tried to be assigned to the embassy in Paris myself, and unable to do so, I decided to run for President.

At New York's Waldorf-Astoria Hotel, the President had a two-hour meeting with Israeli Premier Ben-Gurion.

As the meeting ended, Mr. Kennedy pointed to one of his aides, Myer Feldman, and asked the Premier:

How do you think Mike Feldman would do in a kibbutz?

New York City
May 30, 1961

Merriman Smith has covered the White House for United Press for many years and is considered the dean of White House reporters. At a White House party for newsmen after his Inauguration, President Kennedy took Mr. Smith over to meet Mrs. Kennedy. His introduction went like this:

I want you to met Merriman Smith. We inherited him with the White House.

January 1961

Always youthful in appearance, John F. Kennedy used to enjoy telling his friends of the time when he was a young Senator, waiting in the Senate Office Building elevator, and "some people got into the elevator and asked me for the fourth floor."

A dilemma, it seems to me, is posed by the occasion of a Presidential address to a business group on business conditions less than four weeks after entering the White House, for it is too early to be claiming credit for the new Administration and too late to be blaming the old one.

National Industrial Conference Board
Washington, D. C.
February 13, 1961

One evening, a few weeks after he became President, Mr. Kennedy slipped away from the White House and went to a local movie theater to see "Spartacus."

The President noticed a familiar figure in the row ahead of him. It was the new Secretary of Agriculture, Orville Freeman. The President tapped his Secretary of Agriculture on the shoulder and remarked with a smile:

This is a hell of a way to write a farm program.

Washington, D. C.
January 1961

Shortly after his Inauguration, President Kennedy greeted Madame Hervé Alphand, wife of the French Ambassador, at a White House dinner:

Comment allez-vous? . . . My wife speaks good French, I understand only one out of every five words, but always "de Gaulle."

Washington, D. C.
January 1961

At a Sunday night reception for his new Administration appointees at the White House, Mr. Kennedy remarked to his guests:

The reason for this reception is my desire to see some of the names I have been reading about in the newspaper.

January 1961

Speaking of the Presidency just before his Inauguration, Mr. Kennedy commented:

It's a big job. It isn't going to be so bad. You've got time to think. You don't have all those people bothering you that you had in the Senate—besides, the pay is pretty good.

Georgetown
December 1960

At their Vienna meeting, Premier Khrushchev told President Kennedy:

"You're an old country, we're a young country."
"If you'll look across the table," the forty-four-year-old President quipped, "you'll see that we're not so old."

June 3, 1961

In September, 1960, Mr. Kennedy went to New York to accept the Liberal Party nomination for the Presidency:

I am proud to be the only candidate in 1960 with the nomination of two political parties, although I am not certain how many tickets are now headed in how many states by Senator Goldwater.

Just before you met, a weekly news magazine with a wide circulation featured a section, "Kennedy's Liberal Promises," and described me, and I quote, as "the farthest-out Liberal Democrat around," unquote. While I am not certain of the beatnik definition of "farthest out," I am certain that it was not intended as a compliment.

And last week, as further proof of my credentials, a noted American clergyman was quoted as saying that our society may survive in the event of my election, but it certainly won't be what it was. I would like to think that he was complimenting me, but I'm not sure he was.

Those of you who are here tonight are proof of the fact that some of the best friends the Democrats have are not in the Democratic Party. I think that in November some of them may be in the Republican Party, but I hold out no hope at all for the vast and impressive number of Republicans who suddenly, just before election time— those who are running for office—begin to sound like true Lincolns.

Eight years ago on this occasion, Adlai Stevenson called this quadrennial outburst of affection "the pause in the real Republican occupation known as 'The Liberal Hour,'" and he added, "It should never be confused" (and he was right) "with any period when Congress is in session."

President Kennedy was in rare form when he addressed a White House correspondents' dinner in 1962, shortly after his famous clash with the steel industry over the increase in the price of steel. The increase was eventually cancelled, but only after the President went on national television to bring his case to the people. In his speech before the correspondents, he satirized his own television address:

I have a few opening announcements. First, the sudden and arbitrary action of the officers of this organization in increasing the price of dinner tickets by two dollars and fifty cents over last year constitutes a wholly unjustifiable defiance of the public interest. If this increase is not rescinded but is imitated by the Gridiron, Radio-TV, and other dinners, it will have a serious impact on the entire economy of this city. In this serious hour in our nation's history, when newsmen are awakened in the middle of the night to be given a front page story, when expense accounts are being scrutinized by the Congress, when correspondents are required to leave their families for long and lonely weekends at Palm Beach, the American people will find it hard to accept this ruthless decision made by a tiny handful of executives whose only interest is the pursuit of pleasure. I am hopeful that the Women's Press Club will not join this price rise and will thereby force a rescission.

I'm sure I speak on behalf of all of us in expressing our thanks and very best wishes to Benny Goodman and his group, Gwen Verdon, Miss Sally Ann Howes, and Peter Sellers. I have arranged for them to appear next week on the United States Steel Hour. Actually, I didn't do it. Bobby did it.

Like members of Congress, I have been, during the last few days over the Easter holiday, back in touch with my constituents and seeing how they felt and, frankly, I have come back to Washington from Palm Beach and I'm against my entire program.

I spoke a year ago today at the Inaugural and I would like to paraphrase a couple of statements I made that day by saying that we observe tonight not a celebration of freedom but a victory of party, for we have sworn to pay off the same party debt our forebears ran up nearly a year and three months ago. Our deficit will not be paid off in the next hundred days, nor will it be paid off in the first one thousand days, nor in the life of this administration, or perhaps even in our lifetime on this planet—but let us begin, remembering that generosity is not a sign of weakness and that ambassadors are always subject to Senate confirmation.

For if the Democratic Party cannot be helped by the many who are poor, it cannot be saved by the few who are rich. So let us begin.

Democratic Fund Raising Dinner
January 1962

I have not always considered the membership of the NAM as among my strongest supporters. I'm not sure you have all approached the New Frontier with the greatest possible enthusiasm and I was, therefore, somewhat nervous about accepting this invitation until I did some studying of the history of this organization. I learned that this organization denounced, on one occasion, and I'll quote, "swollen bureaucracy as among the triumphs of Karl Marx" and decried on another occasion new governmental "paternalism and socialism." I was comforted when reading this very familiar language to note that I was in very good company. For the first attack I quoted was on Calvin Coolidge and the second on Herbert Hoover. I remind you of this only to indicate the happy failure of many of our most pessimistic predictions.

National Association of Manufacturers
Convention
December 1961

I want to express my pleasure at this invitation as one whose work and continuity of employment has depended in part upon the union movement.

AFL-CIO Convention
Bal Harbour, Florida
December 1961

This city is no stranger to me. A Parisian designed the city of Washington. He laid out our broad boulevards after living here in this community. When he had finished his generous designs, he presented a bill to the Congress for ninety thousand dollars, and the Congress of the United States, in one of those bursts of economic fervor, for which they are justifiably famous, awarded him the munificent sum of three thousand dollars. Some people have been so unkind as to suggest that your clothes designers have been collecting his bill ever since.

Paris, 1961

Once again Berlin and the Federal Republic have spoiled us for home. Now, when we don't get a million people out for a political speech in Worcester, Massachusetts, or Danbury, Connecticut, everyone, especially the reporters, is going to write that there are signs of apathy in the United States. And when we have crowded dinners of fifty at the White House, I am afraid this dinner is going to throw a pall on the entire affair.

City Hall Luncheon, Berlin, Germany
June 26, 1963

When he visited Germany, President Kennedy was met by enthusiastic crowds, causing him to comment:

Chancellor Adenauer was generous enough to say that the outpouring was spontaneous, and I do believe there was spontaneous good will, but I cannot believe all of those flags they held in their hands came from their rooms and from their houses. As an old politician, somebody must have been working, Mr. Chancellor.

Bonn, Germany
June 23, 1963

In remarks in Bonn, Germany, President Kennedy referred to the fact that German Chancellor Adenauer, one of the world's oldest statesmen, was still very active despite his age:

Carl Schurz wrote in his nineteenth-century memoirs that his first public speech was an extemporaneous, public outburst to a crowd of his fellow students in the great university hall of Bonn.

He related how one of his professors inquired his age and, when told he was nineteen, remarked "Too bad; still too young for our new German Parliament." They have been saying the same thing about your Chancellor for many years.

June 23, 1963

THE
FAMILY

The
Family

There was much discussion after the President appointed his brother Attorney General. Mr. Kennedy recognized the fact that in the beginning many people were against his decision. Shortly after his announcement he joked:

Speaking of jobs for relatives, Master Robert Kennedy, who is four, came to see me today, but I told him we already had an Attorney General.

This district was the first district to endorse me as a candidate for President, nearly a year ago. My family had not even endorsed me when you endorsed me.

Brooklyn, New York
October 27, 1960

I want you to meet my sister, Pat Lawford. She is here for my wife who is home. We are having a baby in November—a boy.

Richmond, California
September 8, 1960

Question: As a Kentuckian, I married a Massachusetts girl. Can you state as evasively as Nixon would under the circumstances, which state, Kentucky or Massachusetts, produces the most beautiful women?

Mr. Kennedy: Taking a leaf out of the Vice President's book, my wife comes from New York and, therefore, I would say that New York produces the most beautifull women.

Louisville, Kentucky
October 5, 1960

When shown a picture of his newest nephew in August, 1963, the President remarked:

He looks like a fine baby—we'll know more later.

Washington, D.C.

In 1944, Mr. Kennedy sent the following note to his younger brother, Bobby, from the Solomon Islands:

The folks sent me a clipping of you taking the oath. The sight of you up there was really moving, particularly as a close examination showed that you have my checked London coat on.

I'd like to know what the hell I'm doing out here while you go stalking around in my drape coat, but I suppose that's what we are out here for, so that our sisters and younger brothers will be safe and secure—frankly, I don't see it that way—at least if you're going to be safe and secure, that's fine with me, but not in my coat, brother.

The Kennedys at Hyannisport in 1960. Standing, left to right: Mrs. Robert Kennedy, Stephen Smith and his wife Jean Kennedy, the President, Robert Kennedy, Patricia Kennedy Lawford, Sargent Shriver, Mrs. Ted Kennedy, and Peter Lawford. Seated: Eunice Kennedy Shriver, Joseph P. Kennedy, Mrs. John F. Kennedy, and Ted Kennedy.

Question: Due to the fact that your wife is going to have a baby and you are certain that it is going to be a boy, there are a lot of expectant fathers who would like to know your secret of knowing that it is going to be a boy.

Mr. Kennedy: She told me. You would have to ask her.

Turlock, California
September 9, 1960

Question: I come from Yonkers. I have an entirely different question to ask tonight, and I think an awful lot of people in this room are interested. Are you hoping it is a boy?

Mr. Kennedy: Well, as a matter of fact, I am flying home tonight to try and find an answer to that question. But actually, I have a daughter, and I know it sounds terrible and treasonous, but I don't really mind having another daughter again if that is the way it goes.

Syracuse, New York
September 29, 1960

I would like to introduce my sister, Eunice Shriver, who lives in Chicago. I have sisters living in all the key electoral states in preparation for this campaign.

Libertyville, Illinois
October 25, 1960

Shortly before an important conference with Secretary of Defense Robert McNamara during the Cuban missile crisis, the President noticed his daughter Caroline running across the White House lawn.

"Caroline," the President shouted, "have you been eating candy?"

There was no answer from the President's young daughter.

"Caroline," the President repeated, "have you been eating candy? Answer yes, no, or maybe."

President Kennedy made a practice of never discussing his official day when he was in his private quarters in the White House with his family.

However, once, a few years after he became President, Mrs. Kennedy asked her husband what kind of day it was.

The President shook his head and mentioned ten things which had gone wrong throughout the morning. "And," he added, "the day is only half over."

On a tour of Fort Bragg to inspect the new United States Special Forces, which had been especially organized for guerilla warfare, Mr. Kennedy noted the green berets that the Special Forces men were wearing and remarked:

I like those berets. The Special Forces need something to make them distinctive. My father even wears one now.

A few days after a national magazine had referred to Bobby Kennedy as "the man with the greatest influence at the

White House," the President received a call in his office from the Attorney General. Turning to a guest as he put his hand over the phone mouthpiece, Mr. Kennedy quipped:

This is the second most powerful man in the nation calling.

Washington, D.C.
June 1961

After he noticed a story in a national magazine which said that the Kennedy brothers were "clothes-conscious," the President telephoned a reporter for the magazine and said:

What do you mean, the clothes-conscious Kennedy

brothers? I may be, but I don't think Bobby is. I don't think Bobby is very well dressed, do you? Why, he still wears those button-down shirts. They went out five years ago. The only people I know who still wear them are Chester [Bowles] and Adlai.

Washington, D. C.
July 1961

Before the members of the City Council of Paris, President Kennedy remarked:

I am the descendant on both sides of two grand-

parents who served in the City Council of Boston, and I am sure they regard that as a more significant service than any of their descendants have yet rendered.

June 2, 1961

I want you to meet my sister, Patricia Lawford, who had the somewhat limited judgment to move from Massachusetts and come to Los Angeles.

Los Angeles, California
September 9, 1960

*John F. Kennedy describing his first meeting at a dinner
with Jacqueline Bouvier (Mrs. Kennedy):*

I leaned across the asparagus and asked her for a date.

I appreciate your being here this morning.
Mrs. Kennedy is organizing herself. It takes her longer
but, of course, she looks better than we do when she does it.

*Fort Worth, Texas
November 1963*

*Addressing a gathering of friends and relatives in Wex-
ford, Ireland, Mr. Kennedy remarked:*

It is my pleasure to be back from whence I came.
Many people are under the impression that all the Kennedys are in Washington, but I am happy to see so many
present who have missed the boat.

June 28, 1963

THE
PRESS
CONFERENCES

The
Press
Conferences

Question: Two books have been written about you recently. One of them has been criticized as being too uncritical of you and the other, by Victor Lasky, as being too critical of you. How would you review them—if you've read them?

President Kennedy: I haven't read all of Mr. Lasky. I've just gotten the flavor of it. I see it's been highly praised by Mr. Drummond, Mr. Krock, and others. I'm looking forward to reading it, because the part that I read was not as brilliant as I gather the rest of it is from what they say about it.

Question: There's a feeling in some quarters, sir, that big business is using the stock market slump as a means of forcing you to come to terms with business. One reputable columnist, after talking to businessmen, obviously, reported this week their attitude is "now we have you where we want you." Have you seen any reflection of this attitude?

President Kennedy: I can't believe I'm where big business wants me.

Question: Mr. President, this being Valentine's Day, sir, do you think it might be a good idea if you would call Senator Strom Thurmond of South Carolina down to the White House for a heart-to-heart talk over what he calls your defeatist foreign policy?

President Kennedy: Well, I think that that meeting should probably be prepared at a lower level.

Question: I wonder if you could tell us whether if you had to do it over again you would work for the Presidency and whether you would recommend the job to others?

President Kennedy: Well, the answer to the first is yes and the answer to the second is no. I don't recommend it to others, at least not for a while.

Question: Mr. President, you once told us you had an opinion as to whether Mr. Nixon should enter the race for the California governorship, but you never did tell us what that was.

President Kennedy: I think I said at the time that I would be glad to confide it to him, and he just has not, as yet, spoken to me about it. I'll be glad to come back to California and talk to him about it.

Question: Mr. President, Congressman Alger of Texas criticized Mr. Salinger as a young and inexperienced White House publicity man, and questioned the advisability of having him visit the Soviet Union. I wonder if you have any comment?

President Kennedy: I know there are always some people who feel that Americans are always young and inexperienced and foreigners are always able and tough and great negotiators. But I don't think that the United States would have acquired its present position of leadership in the free world if that view were correct. Now, he also, as I saw the press, said that Mr. Salinger's main job was to increase my standing in the Gallup polls. Having done that, he's now moving on to improve our communications.

Question: What did you think, sir, of the rather harsh things that Republican Congressman Boyle of Virginia had to say about you and your Press Secretary because Mr. Salinger gave a party last night for his Democratic opponent?

President Kennedy: Well, I can see why he would be quite critical of that. But I will say that I never read as much about a Congressman in the papers as I do about that Congressman and see less legislative results.

Question: Mr. President, last Friday, John Bailey, the Democratic National Chairman made a speech in which he accused Governor Rockefeller of racial prejudice toward Negroes. And I wonder if you felt, even in an election year, that this was a justified statement?

President Kennedy: No, I've never seen any evidence that Mr. Rockefeller is prejudiced in any way toward any racial group, and I'm glad to make that statement, and I'm sure that some of the statements that the Chairman of the Republican Committee has made about me will be similarly repudiated by leading Republicans. I've been waiting for it for about a year and a half.

Question: Mr. President, have you narrowed your search for a new Postmaster General? And are you seeking a man with a business background or a political background?

President Kennedy: The search is narrowing, but we haven't—there are other fields that are still to be considered, including even a postal background.

Question: Mr. President, what is your evaluation of Khrushchev's present status and the nature of the political struggle that is apparently now going on in the Kremlin?

President Kennedy: I would think it is possible that Khrushchev is subjected to the same . . . I don't think we know precisely . . . but I would suppose he has his good months and bad months like we all do.

Question: Mr. President, you have said that you are in favor of the two-term limit to the office of the Presidency. How do you feel about former President Eisenhower's suggestion that the terms of Congressmen also be limited?

President Kennedy: It's the sort of proposal which I may advance in a post-Presidential period, but not right now.